REAL ESTATE HOMEBUYER ESSENTIALS

The Success of Systems and Service

Donna Wysinger

Copyright 2025 © Be a Better Agent

Copyright Notice

Real Estate Homebuyer Essentials:
The Success of Systems and Service
Copyright © 2025 by Be a Better Agent
All rights reserved.

No part of this book may be reproduced, stored in a retrieval system, or transmitted in any form or by any means; electronic, mechanical, photocopying, recording, or otherwise, without prior written permission from the author, except for brief quotations used in a review.

This book is intended for informational and personal use only. The author and publisher are not responsible for any actions or outcomes resulting from the use of the content within. The exercises and prompts are meant to inspire creativity and positive business practices and should not replace professional advice when needed.

ISBN: 979-8-9930660-3-5

Be a Better Agent

For permissions, inquiries, or further information, please email: Donna@BeABetterAgent.com

Dedication

To the buyer advocates, teachers, and colleagues who reminded me that helping someone find a home is both a privilege and a promise ...

Thank you for showing me what true service looks like; steady guidance, clear communication, and care that lasts long after closing. Your wisdom and example shaped the systems and heart behind this book.

To my amazing clients, friends, and family ...

Your trust, loyalty, and referrals have been the foundation of my business and the reason I love what I do. Every search, showing, and set of keys exchanged has been a lesson in patience, purpose, and joy.

This book is for you, and for every buyer who is still out there searching for the place they'll call home.

Thank you.

TABLE OF CONTENTS

INTRODUCTION: *From "Maybe SOMEDAY"*   1
To Keys in Hand
Empower buyers with systems that simplify, support, and lead to success

CHAPTER 1: *ATTRACT & Pre-Qualify*   5
Turning Interest into Intent
Find the right buyers faster and uncover readiness with insight, intention, and care

CHAPTER 2: *The BUYER Consultation*   13
That WINS Trust
Lead with empathy, set expectations early, and earn loyalty through education, not pressure

CHAPTER 3: *MONEY Readiness*   21
Credit Prep & Lender Approval
Turn financial fear into confidence with structure, partnership, and clear communication

CHAPTER 4: *NURTURE Season*   27
Staying Top of Mind
Keep buyers engaged, informed, and inspired while they wait... without the pressure

CHAPTER 5: *SEARCH Strategy*   35
Smart Steps to SUCCESS
Simplify the search, sharpen focus, and help buyers find the home that truly fits

CHAPTER 6: *Showings With PURPOSE*   43
COACHING Decisions On SITE
Transform every showing into a guided discovery that builds confidence and vision

TABLE OF CONTENTS

CHAPTER 7: *Choose and COMMIT*   **51**
Making the OFFER Feel SAFE
Help buyers move from hesitation to action with options, understanding, and trust

CHAPTER 8: *OFFER and Negotiation*   **59**
WIN-WIN Without Overpaying
Negotiate with calm, communicate with confidence, and create solutions that work for everyone

CHAPTER 9: *Under CONTRACT*   **67**
SYSTEMS That SEAL The DEAL
Guide buyers through deadlines and details with steady systems that protect and empower

CHAPTER 10: *Closing, MOVE IN*   **75**
& Your Follow-Up CARE Plan
Celebrate the milestone, strengthen the relationship, and build loyalty that lasts long after move-in day

CONCLUSION: *Buyers for a SEASON*   **81**
Community for a LIFETIME
Keep showing up with gratitude, systems, and service, and watch your clients become your community

MORE MAGIC: *Bonus Materials*   **85**
- Scripts for Soothing Buyers
- Working with Buyers Checklist
- Homebuyer Information Binder
- Moving Made Simple: Agent Edition
- Ideas to Add Extra Heart
- Calming Practices

Foreword

If you've ever guided a buyer through one of the biggest decisions of their life, you know... this business is about far more than homes. It's about people. It's about patience, reassurance, and creating calm where uncertainty lives.

Real estate is personal. Every showing, every conversation, every closing represents a dream in motion. And as agents, we have the privilege of helping bring those dreams to life. But that privilege also carries responsibility: to lead with clarity, compassion, and systems that turn uncertainty into confidence.

This guide was created to help you do exactly that. It's not just about checklists and timelines, it's about trust. It's about building a framework that allows you to serve from a place of peace and professionalism, no matter how unpredictable the market feels. Because when you lead with service and structure, your clients don't just buy a home, they gain an advocate for life.

My wish is that these pages remind you of the heart behind what we do. That you feel seen, supported, and inspired to refine your systems and elevate your service. Whether you've worked with a hundred buyers or you're preparing for your very first, I hope this book feels like a steady hand on your shoulder reminding you: you've got this.

Let's bring calm, confidence, and care to every transaction. And help more buyers find their way home.

Donna Wysinger
Owner/Founder
Be a Better Agent

INTRODUCTION

From "Maybe SOMEDAY" To KEYS in HAND

Less hustle, more heart, more homes.

Buying a home is one of life's biggest adventures. And for many people, one of the most emotional. Excitement, fear, doubt, and hope often live side by side. Between rising rates, market noise, and well-meaning advice from friends and family, today's buyers can feel paralyzed before they even begin. They don't need more data; they need direction.

They need *you*.

I'd like to help you bring calm and confidence to a process that often feels overwhelming. Together, we'll turn chaos into clarity, anxiety into action, and hesitant shoppers into homeowners who feel supported every step of the way.

You'll discover practical systems, thoughtful scripts, and repeatable strategies that make the buyer process smoother for you and simpler for your clients. When you show up with structure and sincerity, your buyers relax and results follow.

🤝 The Purpose & Promise of This Guide

Every great agent learns that **systems** are what create freedom, and **service** is what creates loyalty. This handbook is your framework for both.

You'll learn how to attract qualified buyers, conduct consultations that build trust, and guide clients from pre-approval to closing day with ease. You'll learn how to nurture buyers who aren't quite ready. Because patience and consistency often turn *"not yet"* into *"thank you!"*

My promise is that this guide will help you simplify your buyer process while strengthening your relationships. You'll gain the language, tools, and confidence to stay calm under pressure, keep in touch during long timelines, and deliver a buying experience so good that clients can't help but tell their friends.

Understanding Today's Buyer Mindset 🧠

Let's be real: today's buyers are scared. They scroll headlines about interest rates, see homes selling, and wonder if they've missed their chance. Many first-time buyers question whether they'll ever afford a home, while seasoned buyers wrestle with the logistics of selling and buying at the same time. **Your role isn't to talk them out of fear. It's to walk them through it.**

Education, empathy, and options are your superpowers. When you listen deeply, explain clearly, and present choices, fear fades and trust takes root. Your calm, informed guidance helps buyers see what's possible. And when clients  feel empowered, they act with confidence. And that's when everything changes.

 How to Use This Guidebook

This isn't a textbook; it's a toolkit. Each chapter walks you step-by-step through the buyer journey; from the first inquiry to post-closing follow-up, complete with scripts, checklists, and resources you can customize for your own business.

Included are quick quotes, pro tips, and real-world reminders from one agent to another. At the end of every chapter, you'll find **Key Reflections**, designed to help you pause and personalize what you've learned before moving forward. The goal is for knowledge to become mastery.

Your Buyer-First Pledge

As professionals, we wear many hats; educator, counselor, advocate, problem-solver, cheerleader, and sometimes even therapist. Your Buyer-First Pledge is a reminder of what matters most: the people behind the paperwork.

- **Consistency**: Buyers need steady communication. Check in even when nothing new has happened. It builds confidence.
- **Transparency**: Be clear, honest, and realistic. Simplify complex steps and empower your clients with understanding.
- **Advocacy**: Protect their interests like your own. Every call, contract, and closing table moment matters.
- **Care**: Because long after they forget the transaction details, they'll remember how you made them feel.

When you lead with clarity, confidence, and compassion, you don't just sell homes, you build trust, change lives, and create a business that feels good to run.

A Final Thought Before We Begin

Every buyer journey is unique, but the heartbeat is always the same: a dream, a doorway, and a person brave enough to take the first step. You're the guide who helps them cross that threshold.

Let's get started.

Your next loyal buyer is waiting for a calm, confident agent like you.

CHAPTER 1

ATTRACT & Pre-Qualify
Turning Interest into Intent

Every great buyer journey begins with curiosity. A neighbor walks through your open house *"just to look."* A past client messages you about a friend who's thinking of buying. A new lead comes through your website, social post, or referral. In that instant, your goal isn't to close them. It's to connect with them.

> *Real estate success = taking care of and valuing the customer.*

When you treat every first interaction as the start of a relationship, not a transaction, you create the space for trust to grow. And trust is what transforms casual curiosity into committed clients.

⚙ Lead Sources & Follow-Up Workflows

Your best leads come from the places where your presence already feels genuine. For some agents, that's open houses; for others, it's SOI *(sphere of influence)* referrals, social media DMs, or community events. Whatever your channels, the key is speed and sincerity.

Respond Quickly, Warmly, and With Purpose.

If a message arrives during business hours, aim to reply within an hour. Your tone should be friendly and helpful, not salesy or scripted. Something as simple as:

"Hi [Name]! I'm so glad you reached out. I'd love to help you start mapping out your home search. Can we hop on a quick 15-minute call to learn more about your timeline and goals?"

Every interaction should do two things: 1) help the buyer feel heard, and 2) clearly outline what happens next. The sooner you provide a next step, the less likely the lead is to drift away.

Create a "Fast Follow Up" System:

- **Inbound Lead**: Immediate text or call → add to CRM → send a link to your *Discovery Form* or *Request for Information*.
- **Open House**: Within 24 hours, thank them, offer a *"Buyers' Guide PDF,"* and ask if they'd like a quick market overview.

- **Referral**: Personalize your outreach: *"Melanie said wonderful things about you! I'd love to learn what you're looking for."*
- **Social DM**: Move them to a call or consult quickly; *"Let's set up a quick chat to get you clarity on next steps."*

Fast follow up says: *I'm here, I care, and I'm prepared.*

Preliminary 3-Question Check

Before you dive into home searches or pre-approvals, take a moment to collect three key details, the foundation for your **Homebuyer Summary**.

- **Timing**: *"When do you ideally hope to move?"*
    - Helps you gauge urgency and pacing.
- **Financing:** Have you spoken with a lender yet, or would you like a trusted introduction?
    - Opens the door to talk about comfort ranges instead of intimidating numbers.
- **Motivation**: What's prompting your move?
    - This one's gold. Their *"why"* reveals everything about their energy, flexibility, and follow through.

These three questions help you assess readiness in minutes. They also set the stage for a meaningful consultation later. You already understand their story.

Homebuyer Barometer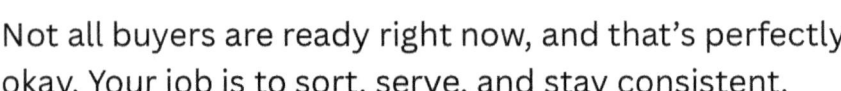

Not all buyers are ready right now, and that's perfectly okay. Your job is to sort, serve, and stay consistent.

Category: HOT

Description: Pre-approved and ready to tour within 30 days.

Next Steps: Book consultation + showings, weekly updates.

Category: WARM

Description: 30–90 days out. Exploring homes or getting finances in order, preparing current home for sale.

Next Steps: lender connection, alerts set up, weekly check-ins.

Category: NURTURE

Description: 90+ days or still dreaming.

Next Steps: Add to long-term nurture sequence with informational, light touches *(twice monthly emails or postcards)*.

Buyers may move between these stages. Your system simply ensures they never fall through the cracks.

Tools That Keep You Ready

Quick-Qualification Script: Use this short, conversational framework when a lead comes in:

"I'd love to learn a little about your plans so we can create the best strategy together.
- *When are you hoping to move?*
- *Have you talked to a lender yet, or would you like a referral?*
- *And tell me what's prompting your move; a change, a dream, or something new on the horizon?"*

Discovery Form: A simple, branded digital form that captures their answers and auto-tags them in your CRM *(Customer Relationship Management)* system. Keep it simple. You'll receive more responses.

CRM Tags & Automations: Set up workflows for Hot, Warm, and Nurture buyers. Each should have distinct follow-up rhythms, templates, and reminders. Automation doesn't mean impersonal. **It means consistent care even when you're busy.**

The Homebuyer Summary

The **Homebuyer Summary** is your command center for organization. Think of it as an overview of your clients, that keeps every key detail of your buyer relationship right where you need it. When you have dozens of conversations, listings, buyer leads, and follow-ups in motion, this summary becomes your client anchor.

It's more than just a contact record; it's a reflection of your professionalism and care. At a glance, you can see who your buyer is, where they are in the process, and what they need next. It keeps you proactive instead of reactive, and prevents the small but important details, like lender updates or personal milestones, from being missed.

Include the Essentials:

- **Contact details and lead source** – so you can thank referrers and track what's working.
- **Their *"why now"* and desired timeline** – this is the emotional heartbeat of every purchase; it keeps your guidance personal, not generic.
- **Financing status and lender contact** – ensures smooth communication and avoids last-minute surprises.
- **Notes from your consult or Discovery Form** – what they value most, what they fear, and what would make this move feel successful.
- **Specifics desired** – location, property size, style, price range, monthly payment *(must haves and would likes)*.
- **Follow-up schedule and milestones** – key dates, check-ins, and status changes to keep momentum moving.

This simple sheet can live in your CRM, inside your buyer folder, or printed in your showing binder; anywhere you'll actually see and use it.

Having it all in one glance doesn't just make you look and feel organized, it creates clients that feel like they are the most important. And that, more than any system or script, is what turns satisfied buyers into lifelong advocates.

🔑 Key Reflections

How can I make my first interaction feel more personal and less transactional?

_____
_____
_____
_____
_____

Which part of my follow-up system needs tightening; response time, CRM tagging, or nurture rhythm?

_____
_____
_____
_____
_____

What's one piece of value I could share with every new lead this month?

_____
_____
_____
_____
_____

NOTES

CHAPTER 2

The BUYER Consultation
That WINS Trust

The **buyer consultation** is where calm replaces confusion. It's where you transform anxious questions into confident decisions. And where your professionalism quietly sets you apart.

Set expectations, reduce fear, and earn commitment.

In a world of instant listings, online opinions, and constant noise, your consultation brings focus and trust back into the process. Buyers finally have a guide, not just a gatekeeper. When you approach this meeting as an act of service and not a sales pitch, you'll feel the shift. They stop comparing agents and start connecting with you. And **when connection happens, confidence follows, opening the door to collaboration, clarity, and a relationship built on genuine trust.**

📅 Your Consultation Agenda

Your consultation is not about memorizing a script. It's about guiding a clear, reassuring conversation that gives your clients a roadmap and a reason to commit. Keep it simple and structured.

Welcome & Goals

Start with heart. Ask: *"What would make this move a big win for you?"* Let them talk. You'll hear motivation, fears, and priorities; the foundation for everything ahead.

Process Map

Show the full journey from *Consult → Keys in Hand*. Use a simple visual or handout to explain each stage: pre-approval, search, offer, negotiation, under contract, and closing. When they can see the process, it helps fade the fear.

Market Truth

Give them a reality check wrapped in reassurance. *"Inventory is tight right now, but preparation beats panic."* Frame facts as tools, not threats.

Timeline

Outline what's typical and where flexibility matters. Set expectations about home searches, offer response times, and closing windows.

Money Talk

Ease into the topic. Replace *"How much can you afford?"* with *"What monthly payment feels comfortable?"* Encourage lender conversations early, but keep *your* focus on emotional comfort, not financial jargon.

Roles & Responsibilities

Clarify how you will work together. *"I'll handle the details and guide your decisions, but you'll always stay in control."* This transparency builds immediate trust.

Next Steps

Always close with clear action: lender intro, portal and searches setup, or first showing appointments date. End with confidence: *"I am going to share what will happen next so you always know where we are."*

First-Time Buyer Myth-Busters

You'll hear the same myths again and again. And every time, you have the chance to educate and empower. A few key ones to manage:

- **Myth 1**: *"I need 20% down to buy a home."*
  → Explain that many buyers purchase with far less through well-structured programs.

- **Myth 2**: *"I should wait until rates drop."*
  → Share that rates fluctuate constantly. The right time to buy is when the life move makes sense. Homeowners can choose to refinance when/if rates go down.

- **Myth 3**: *"The inspection and appraisal are the same thing."*
  → Clarify the difference: one protects the buyer's awareness, the other protects the lender's investment.
- **Myth 4**: *"If I find the home online, I don't need an agent."*
  → Smile and say, *"That's like self-diagnosing on Google. It's possible, though not recommended."*

When you bust myths with warmth and humor, you replace fear with understanding. And understanding breeds loyalty.

Buyer Process Rules and Mechanics

Set these boundaries early and with kindness. They'll prevent chaos later.

- **Showings**: Explain how scheduling works, why flexibility helps, and how to show respect when visiting homes.
- **Safety**: Always have a plan. Encourage daylight showings when possible, and remind clients you'll guide the process.
- **Decision Rules**: Teach your buyers how to decide, not just what to choose. Help them rate homes objectively *(layout, light, location)* so emotion doesn't overshadow reason.

- **Offer Mechanics**: Outline how offers work in your market; what *"earnest money," "contingencies,"* and *"terms"* mean. When they understand the structure, they can act quickly and with confidence when the right home appears.

Tools That Build Trust

These are your trust accelerators: small touches that turn confusion into clarity. Have one or more of these designed and branded and ready for your consultations.

- **Slide Deck Outline**: A visual version of your process for in-person or Zoom consultations.
- **"What to Expect" Handout**: Step-by-step timeline with key milestones, kept light and visual.
- **Commitment to Work Together Form *(Buyer Broker Agreement)***: Presented confidently, not as pressure, but as partnership. *"This agreement simply confirms I'll be representing your best interests every step of the way."*

A great consultation begins with connection. When buyers leave your meeting feeling understood, informed, and supported, they'll move forward with confidence and loyalty.

 **PRO TIP** Confidence isn't loud. It's calm, prepared, and consistent. Your systems and processes are what build trust before the first showing even begins.

🗝️ Key Reflections

How can I make my consultation feel less like a presentation and more like a conversation?

_____
_____
_____
_____
_____

What tool or takeaway could make my consultation unforgettable for every new buyer?

_____
_____
_____
_____
_____

Which myth do I hear most often? And how can I explain it with empathy and ease?

_____
_____
_____
_____
_____
_____

NOTES

DOODLES

CHAPTER 3
MONEY Readiness
Credit Prep & Lender Approval

You are a resource, not a sales person.

Money talk can stir up stress. But when you bring structure and empathy, it turns into empowerment. Your role is to replace guesswork with guidance and help your clients move from a wishful budget to a workable plan.

Money is emotional. It touches dreams, self-worth, and sometimes even old stories about what's *"possible."* When you approach these with patience and understanding, you ease buyers' concerns. Instead of pressure, you offer partnership; a calm, step-by-step approach that helps them make confident decisions about one of the biggest investments of their lives. Choices get clearer, and progress feels possible. **That's the gift of financial confidence. And you're the one who helps them find it.**

Your Lender Partners 🏠

You don't need a dozen lenders. You need a small circle of trusted partners who communicate clearly and treat your clients with care. A good lender relationship feels like teamwork. You each play a vital role in keeping buyers informed and calm from pre-approval to closing.

Your standards matter. Choose lenders who:

- Respond quickly to both you and your clients.
- Provide weekly updates while under contract.
- Call or text when milestones are reached *(pre-approval issued, appraisal ordered, clear to close)*.
- Match your tone of reassurance and professionalism.

Your **Lender Partner Menu** should include 2–3 reliable contacts with different specialties *(first-time buyers, investment properties, or local credit unions)*. Present them as options, not obligations. So, buyers will always feel empowered to choose.

> *"I work with a few excellent lenders who share my communication style. I'm happy to introduce you so you can compare and find your best fit."*

This makes you a resource, not a salesperson, and that difference builds instant trust.

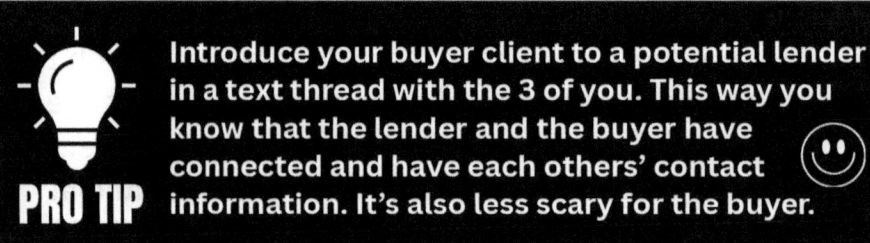

PRO TIP: Introduce your buyer client to a potential lender in a text thread with the 3 of you. This way you know that the lender and the buyer have connected and have each others' contact information. It's also less scary for the buyer.

Pre-Approval vs. Pre-Qualification

Buyers hear these terms everywhere, but rarely know what they mean. This is your moment to bring understanding.

- **Pre-Qualification** is a quick estimate based on self-reported information. It's a starting point, not a promise.
- **Pre-Approval** means the lender has verified income, credit, and assets. It's stronger and far more reliable when it's time to make an offer.

Encourage your buyers to obtain a fully underwritten pre-approval when possible. It strengthens their position and shortens stress later.

Then, introduce the basics of rate and fee comparison:

- **Rates can shift daily**. Timing and credit make a difference.
- **Points, credits, and fees vary**. Encourage them to review the *Loan Estimate* carefully.
- **The lowest rate isn't always the best fit** if the service or timeline causes delays.

Your job isn't to interpret numbers; it's to help clients understand the process so they feel secure asking the right questions.

Credit Tune-Ups & Savings Plans 🐖

Sometimes, buyers aren't ready. And that's okay. You can still serve them with grace and structure. Offer encouragement and a path forward with the lender you connected your buyers with so they can work toward the ability to obtain a loan and purchase a home:

- **Review their credit** and outline a plan to improve it and become ready to buy.
- **Suggest small wins**: reducing balances, paying on time, avoiding new accounts.
- **Help them design a Savings Plan** for a down payment and closing costs. Even a simple monthly target creates momentum.
- **Discuss gift funds** and down-payment assistance programs *(DPA)* in general terms, then refer them to their lender for specifics.

The key is to help buyers see possibility instead of pressure. A three-month or six-month plan with tangible goals feels hopeful, not hard.

> *"Let's make a plan for your 'ready' moment. You don't have to do everything today, just the next right thing."*

🧮 Tools That Build Confidence

Budget & Payment Comfort Calculator

This tool reframes affordability from *"What can I qualify for?"* to *"What feels right?"* Encourage buyers to identify their sleep-at-night number; the payment amount that brings peace, not panic.

Lender Intro Email Template

A short, professional message you can personalize:

> **Subject**: I Have a Buyer That Would Love to Talk with You About Loan Options
>
> Hi [Lender's Name],
>
> I'd like to introduce you to [Buyer Name]. They're exploring their home-buying options and would love your guidance on pre-approval and next steps.
>
> [Buyer Name], [Lender] is one of my trusted partners who communicates clearly and always takes great care of clients. You're in good hands!
>
> Warmly,
>
> [Your Name]

Quick intros like this keep momentum going, and position you as the steady connector at the center of your buyers' team.

Script: Define the "Sleep-at-Night" Number

> *"Instead of focusing on the maximum amount you could borrow, let's define the number that helps you sleep well at night. That's your true comfort zone, and where smart, happy decisions live."*

This line reframes fear into empowerment and turns a stressful topic into a self-care moment.

🔑 Key Reflections

Which lender partners truly align with my communication style and values?

_____
_____
_____
_____
_____

How can I simplify the money talk to reduce stress and build trust?

_____
_____
_____
_____
_____

What follow-up system can I use to keep financing milestones on track?

_____
_____
_____
_____
_____
_____

CHAPTER **4**

NURTURE Season
Staying Top of Mind

Some buyers are ready today. Some are not. And that's okay.

The time between *"We'd love to buy someday"* and *"We're ready to write an offer"* is where loyalty is built. It's where buyers watch, learn, and decide who they trust to guide them when the timing is right. How you show up during this in-between season; steady, consistent, and caring, determines whether you'll be their first call or a distant memory in their inbox.

Nurture Season involves the art of being present without pressure, of offering value, insight, and encouragement while allowing buyers the breathing room they need. Over time, your gentle consistency becomes the reassurance they didn't even know they desired. You're not just staying top-of-mind, you're earning a place in their circle of confidence.

The Purpose of the Nurture Arc

Think of your follow-up process as a **Nurture Arc,** a guided, thoughtful rhythm that provides value over time. Each touchpoint builds familiarity and reassurance. You're not reminding them that you exist; you're reminding them that you care.

Design a flow that spans 30, 60, and 90+ days, blending education and encouragement along the way. The tone? Light, positive, helpful; never pushy.

Example Nurture Arc:

- **Day 1 – 7**: Thank-you message with a *"Homebuying Roadmap"* or local lender introduction.
- **Day 14**: Text or email, *"Here's one quick tip to help you prep for pre-approval."*
- **Day 30**: Market update plus small success story: *"Here's how one couple found their home when they thought they couldn't."*
- **Day 60**: Email or postcard, *"3 Simple Ways to Build Your Down Payment Faster."*
- **Day 90**: *"Ready-When-You-Are"* note with a cheerful check-in and next-step invite.

Simple, kind, and purposeful touches make people feel supported, not sold. You can modify the above example to allow weekly or bi-weekly connections. And be sure to *have a checklist for your follow-up sequence so every potential buyer receives the same, high-care service.*

III. Content Pillars that Build Trust

When you're planning your follow-up content, think in pillars; a few key themes you rotate through so your messages always feel balanced, supported, and relevant.

Market Micro-Updates
Keep buyers informed without overwhelming them. Share short, digestible insights: *"Rates nudged down a bit this week,"* or *"Inventory ticked up. More options on the way!"* Small truths feel trustworthy.

Affordability Tactics
Show buyers creative, real-world solutions: lender programs, credits, budgeting ideas, or cost-saving strategies. Keep it broad, friendly, and compliant. Your goal is empowerment, not advice.

"House Anatomy" Lessons
Teach simple elements about homes: roof age, foundation tips, energy efficiency, inspections. Educational content positions you as a calm expert, not a salesperson.

Success Stories
Share wins from other clients, especially those who started out nervous or unsure. Real stories give hope and remind buyers what is possible.

When your messages **teach, encourage, and inspire,** buyers look forward to hearing from you.

Cadence & Channels

Variety keeps things human. Mix your methods: texts, emails, short videos, branded informational postcards, and even handwritten notes.

Text: Quick, friendly check-ins like, *"Saw a great article on first-time buyers and thought of you!"*

Email: Short, formatted messages with one clear point and a helpful takeaway.

Video Drops: A 60-second selfie video can create more connection than 10 typed paragraphs. Try: *"Hi [Name], I wanted to share a quick buyer tip today about what to do before you fall in love with a house."*

Micro-Check-Ins: Occasional messages just to say hello, congratulate them on progress, or share a new resource.

Consistency matters more than frequency. One authentic touch once or twice a month builds more loyalty than five automated emails that sound generic.

Tools to Streamline Your System

90-Day Nurture Calendar
A simple printable planner that outlines when and how to reach out. Break it down into four weekly categories: education, encouragement, inspiration, and invitation.

Template Library
Save your favorite texts, emails, and social posts so you can reuse them with ease. Personalize them each time, but never start from scratch.

12 Micro-Video Ideas

Short scripts or prompts you can record in one sitting; topics like:

- *"The 3 Most Common First-Time Buyer Questions"*
- *"What to Expect After Pre-Approval"*
- *"What Happens Between Offer and Keys"*

Ready-When-You-Are Planner

This will help you track each buyer's stage and next steps during their Nurture Season. Include:

- Buyer name, contact information, and approximate ready date.
- Financing or pre-approval status.
- Last contact date + next follow-up reminder.
- Notes on current fears, hesitations, or wins.
- Checklist for your follow-up connections.

Keeping your planner's pages updated turns uncertainty into strategy. You'll always know exactly who to reach out to and what to say when you do.

These tools make your follow up feel organized, thoughtful, and easy to sustain, so your energy stays high, not drained.

PRO TIP — Silence creates doubt. A two-line text sent with care can rebuild momentum faster than a perfect email sent too late.

🔑 Key Reflections

How can I add more heart to my follow up without adding more hours to my week?

_____
_____
_____
_____
_____

What stories or lessons could inspire my buyers during their wait time before buying?

_____
_____
_____
_____
_____

Which tools can I set up today to make consistency effortless tomorrow?

_____
_____
_____
_____
_____

NOTES

DOODLES

CHAPTER 5

SEARCH Strategy
Smart Steps To SUCCESS

From infinite feeds to a focused list.

Once buyers are pre-approved and emotionally ready, the search begins, and this is where overwhelm often sneaks in. Between endless online listings, unsolicited *"dream home"* texts from friends, and social media highlight reels, buyers can quickly lose focus.

Your job is to bring them back to center. A smart search strategy helps clients trade scrolling for strategy and adds filters for focus. You're not just showing homes; you're curating their experience, helping them see what truly fits instead of what merely looks exciting.

When you help buyers define their *"musts," "maybes,"* and *"never-evers,"* everything becomes easier. They stop chasing listings and start noticing patterns. They begin to trust the process... and they begin to trust *you*.

◎ The Power of Priorities

Before you open a single portal, define the target. Encourage buyers to separate needs from wants by creating a **Buyer Criteria Matrix**. This exercise grounds the search in reality while keeping it personal and flexible.

Must-Haves are non-negotiables. These are items that define their quality of life.

 Example: 3 bedrooms, main-level laundry, fenced yard for the dog.

Nice-to-Haves are preferences that can shift if the home checks most other boxes.

 Example: Open floor plan, large pantry, or finished basement.

Deal-Breakers are the boundaries. They are the items that would make your buyers unhappy no matter how pretty the kitchen is.

 Example: Too much road noise, small yard, or HOA restrictions.

Layer in **commute and lifestyle filters**. Ask questions like:

> "What does your perfect weekday morning look like?" or "How long do you want your drive to feel?"

When you connect their lifestyle vision to their search filters, you create emotional alignment, not just data alignment.

Smart Portal Setup

Most buyers love searching online, but it's your job to turn that habit into a system. Set up a search portal with custom parameters that match their **Buyer Criteria Matrix**. Too broad, and they'll drown in listings. Too narrow, and they'll feel like there's nothing out there.

Tips for Smart Setup:

- Start broad, then refine after the first few tours. Consider your first showing day as more of a fact-finding mission. What do they really like and desire? Going through the first few homes and asking questions can give you a lot more information than you received at the initial consultation appointment.
- Use map polygons to focus on specific lifestyle areas like parks, schools, trails, or commute zones.
- Set alert frequency on your searches to *"daily"* or immediate for hot markets.
- Encourage them to *"heart"* or *"favorite"* listings they like and leave comments in the app for shared notes.
- Explain that portals don't always tell the whole story. Some homes sell before they appear online. That's why your relationship and network still matter.

PRO TIP: Send all search results to yourself first. Then review and send along only the properties you know your buyers will love. That way, just the best ones make it through, and your clients will learn to trust your instincts and your expertise even more!

🔍 Previewing Like a Pro

A great buyer doesn't just see listings, they evaluate them. Teach clients how to preview homes efficiently so they save time and emotional energy.

Drive-By Previews

Encourage buyers to do quick drive-bys before setting showing appointments. They'll get a sense of the neighborhood, street traffic, and vibe. Often, this alone helps narrows their list. Explain to your buyers that it's important to honor homeowners' time *(and of course, the buyers and your time as well)*. You don't want to set appointments and then have your buyers unwilling to get out of the car at a property that looked a whole lot better online.

Google Street Views & Parcel Research

Encourage your clients to do some Google Maps *(yellow pegman)* reconnaissance. A few clicks can reveal lot shape, slope, nearby structures, or views that photos hide. It's a small *(and fun)* step that adds massive context.

Read the Disclosures

Coach them on reviewing property details early; age of roof, furnace, HOA fees, known issues. This prevents surprises and helps them focus on homes that align with their goals and budget.

When buyers learn to screen homes through a pro lens, they begin to feel empowered and informed.

Tools That Keep You Organized

Buyer Criteria Matrix
A simple, printable grid where buyers list their Must-Haves, Nice-to-Haves, and Deal-Breakers. Revisit this after every few showings. It helps clients stay grounded as preferences evolve.

"First-Pass Filter" Worksheet
A quick checklist for pre-screening properties before touring. Include prompts like:

- Does it meet at least 3 of your 4 must-haves?
- Can you see yourself living here for 3–5 years?
- Did you find anything that gives you pause?

When buyers use this worksheet before showings, their decisions become faster and more confident.

Home Comparison Grid
When buyers see multiple homes in one day, memories blur. The Grid helps them separate feeling from fact. After each showing, rate the home *(1-10)* on:

- Layout & Function   6   9   4   8
- Neighborhood
- Condition
- Price/Value
- *"Feels Like Home"* Factor

Review scores together. Patterns will emerge, helping them move from *"We like them all!"* to *"This one's the winner."*

> **"The right home isn't the one that checks every box. It's the one that fits your life and your comfort zone."**

🗝️ Key Reflections

How can I help buyers connect their lifestyle goals to their search filters?

_____
_____
_____
_____

What step could make my showing days more focused and less frantic?

_____
_____
_____
_____

How can I easefully remind buyers that finding *"the one"* is about alignment, not perfection?

_____
_____
_____
_____
_____

NOTES

DOODLES

CHAPTER 6

Showings With PURPOSE
COACHING Decisions On SITE

"Coaching" your buyers creates a partnership.

For buyers, showings are where dreams start to feel real and where overwhelm can creep in fast. The flood of smells, colors, comments, and *"what-ifs"* can turn excitement into confusion if there's no system guiding the experience.

Your role is to bring structure to the swirl. When every showing day has a clear purpose, you transform *"just another look"* into a confident step toward home.

The goal isn't to rush decisions; it's to help clients recognize rightness when it appears. Showings are a chance to teach your buyers how to think like homeowners, not house hunters.

 **The 3-Layer Tour:**
Big Rocks → Systems → Details

A purposeful showing unfolds in layers, each one building on the last.

Layer 1: Big Rocks
Start with the broad strokes: location, lot, light, and layout. These are the unchangeables — the things that define a home's daily comfort.

Ask, *"Can you picture your life flowing easily through this space?"*

Layer 2: Systems
Once the big picture fits, shift to function. Review what you can observe: roof age, windows, HVAC vents and flow, water heater access, drainage. You're not the inspector, but you're coaching awareness. Point out what to note and what to verify later.

Layer 3: Details
Finally, zoom in. Storage, outlets, windows, finishes, yard usability, traffic noise, interior traffic flow, and curb appeal. Remind buyers that details can be improved, but the bones must feel right.

This approach keeps emotion grounded in structure. It prevents "shiny object" distractions and creates natural decision checkpoints.

Teaching Buyers How to Look

Buyers often focus on décor, not durability. Most items that distract are cosmetic. We know that staging helps sell homes. And we want our clients to see a property and get excited and see themselves living there.

Aaaaand... we need to make sure our clients are gently redirected to notice what matters when it comes to making decisions:

- **Condition Clues**: water stains, uneven floors, window seals, musty smells.
- **Red Flags**: active leaks, foundation cracks, major DIY electrical.
- **Renovation Realism**: small fixes vs. costly surprises.

Empower them to use all senses. Encourage notes and photos of concerns. Teach them to look through the staging to the structure underneath. The more they learn, the more confident and loyal they become.

> *"Every home tells a story. Our job is to read it together before we decide if it's a tale worth continuing."*

 The Debrief Method

Right after each showing, before phones buzz and memories fade, pause curbside for a quick debrief. Ask three things:

- **1–10 Rating**: *"On a scale of one to ten, where does this one land?"*

- **Top 3 Pros & Cons**: one positive for each concern.
- **Deal-Breaker Check**: *"Anything here that instantly takes this home off the list?"*

Capture notes immediately. Buyers love seeing you treat their feedback like data. Over time, patterns will emerge that lead naturally to the right choice.

In today's market, it's easy for buyers to lose heart when they can't find what they love, or when their offers aren't accepted right away. Discouragement can cloud decision-making, and they may start second guessing themselves or circling back to homes they already ruled out.

Kindly guide them to stay focused on their original *Must Haves* and *Deal Breakers*. Remind them that the right home will meet their core needs, not just their current emotions. This helps them stay grounded, confident, and forward moving, saving everyone time, energy, and frustration.

Once they've shared their impressions and you've helped them realign with their priorities, gently close the loop with a clear next step:

> *"Let's decide whether to <u>advance</u> this one or <u>release</u> it before we leave. That way we only carry forward what truly fits."*

Mindset Reset: Stay the Course

The right home won't ask your buyers to compromise on what truly matters. When they start to lose hope or revisit old *"maybes,"* remind them: every *"no"* brings them closer to their *"yes."* Your calm consistency keeps them grounded and focused, even when the market tests their patience.

 **Tools for the Road**

Showing Day Packet
A folder or digital file with property sheets, notes, disclosures, and a quick-rating chart. Add neighborhood amenities, drive times, and safety reminders.

Neighborhood Snapshot
A single-page summary of local highlights; parks, schools, eateries, walkability score, commute notes. This way your buyers visualize lifestyle, not just layout.

Digital Note App or Clipboard
Encourage buyers to jot short impressions after each tour. A few words now prevent *"Was that the blue house or the brick one?"* later.

- Property address & MLS number
- 1–10 rating
- Top 3 pros and cons
- Deal breaker noted *(Y/N)*
- Space for next-step decision: Advance / Release

By tracking impressions, you help buyers make decisions logically, not emotionally. Then reviewing all the notes together paints a clear picture of priorities. You'll want to keep showings to eight or less in a day to prevent overwhelm and buyers forgetting what they saw and liked.

 **PRO TIP** Stay silent for the first sixty seconds inside each home. Let buyers absorb the space before offering input. The pause lets them feel ownership, and gives *you* insight into their instincts.

🗝 Key Reflections

How can I make each showing feel like a guided discovery, not a whirlwind?

_____
_____
_____
_____

What simple cues can I use to help buyers notice condition and not just décor?

_____
_____
_____
_____

How will I document feedback so every tour builds toward clarity and confidence?

_____
_____
_____
_____
_____

NOTES

DOODLES

CHAPTER 7

Choose and COMMIT
Making the OFFER Feel SAFE

This is the moment your buyers have been working toward, and it is the one they often fear the most. After weeks or months of research, tours, and *"almosts,"* suddenly it's time to make a real move. Excitement mixes with anxiety, and every *"what if"* in the book starts to surface.

Preparation turns pressure into power.

Your job is to bring calm to the crossroad. Decision-making doesn't have to feel pressured; it can feel *protected*. When you help buyers see that their offer is not a leap of faith but a step of confidence, everything changes. You're not just writing contracts, you're building courage.

 The Decision Triangle:
Need Fit + Financial Fit + Feel Fit

At this stage, emotion and logic finally meet. The **Decision Triangle** keeps buyers balanced between head, heart, and home.

Need Fit
Does the home meet their Must Haves, respect their Deal Breakers, and align with their lifestyle priorities? If it checks those boxes, the foundation is strong.

Financial Fit
Is the purchase within their *"sleep-at-night"* comfort zone? Review payment estimates, taxes, HOA dues, and any renovation costs to ensure peace of mind.

Feel Fit
Sometimes a home just feels right. Encourage them to notice how their body and energy respond when they walk through it. Do they relax, smile, imagine themselves living there?

When all three sides align; need, numbers, and feeling, it's a green light. And when one side wobbles, your job isn't to talk them into it, but to talk them through it.

Offer Strategy Levers

Every offer has moving parts, and understanding those levers helps buyers feel in control. When clients see that they have options, fear gives way to empowerment.

- **Price** – The headline number that opens the door. Discuss strategy, not emotion.
- **Terms** – Earnest money, financing type, appraisal gap coverage, closing timeline.
- **Timing** – Flexibility often wins over dollars; align with the seller's needs when possible.
- **Inclusions** – Personal property, warranties, or rent-backs can sweeten the deal.
- **Contingencies** – Inspection, appraisal, or sale contingencies must be managed with transparency and timing.

> *"Your offer is more than a number, it's a package of trust, timing, and insight."*

Create a simple **Offer Options Side-by-Side** table so buyers can visualize different combinations.

 Framing Risk and "If-Then" Pathways

Even confident buyers worry about what-ifs. Your job is to frame those risks into clear, rational choices. Instead of saying, *"There's always a risk,"* try:

"Here's what happens if the appraisal comes in low… and here's our plan <u>then</u>."

"If the seller counters, then we'll revisit your comfort zone and adjust strategically."

When you outline *"If-Then"* pathways, uncertainty becomes preparation. **You shift the conversation from fear of loss to power of choice.**

Remember: reassurance doesn't mean removing risk, it means illuminating the path through it.

Scripts for Confidence

"Here are three ways we can win without regret."

> *"Option one: Write strong and clean to lead with certainty.*
>
> *"Option two: Write solid and flexible to stay competitive but cautious.*
>
> *"Option three: Write safely with contingencies and shorter terms to stay in play."*

Give buyers language that matches their personality. Some need bold encouragement; others need gentle pacing.

The win isn't always *"getting the house."* Sometimes the win is *feeling at peace* with the decision, no matter the outcome.

Tools That Support Decision Direction

Offer Options Side-by-Side
Visually compare multiple offer versions; price, terms, and risk levels. Seeing it side by side removes confusion and makes logic visible.

Buyer Net Estimate

Provide a simple summary showing estimated payment, closing costs, and total cash to close. When the math is transparent, anxiety decreases and trust deepens.

Offer Prep Checklist

Create a form that keeps both you and your buyers organized, informed, and ready for action. It's your pre-flight plan: a simple tool that ensures every document is reviewed, every question is answered, and every decision maker feels confident before signatures hit the page. It includes items like verifying pre-approval, confirming proof of funds, reviewing your **Side-by-Side Offer Options**, and discussing any *"If-Then"* scenarios that may arise during negotiations.

Having a checklist ready means no last-minute surprises or frantic scrambles. Instead, you'll lead your clients through the process feeling prepared, protected, and proud of the offer they're making.

❋ You Are the Master

Your calm confidence is the anchor buyers need most. You've guided them through uncertainty, taught them how to evaluate risk, and helped them recognize what "ready" truly feels like. Now, your steady presence turns decision making into empowerment.

A strong offer isn't about luck or leverage, it's about alignment. When the home meets their needs, fits their finances, and feels right, the *"yes"* comes naturally. Your role is to keep the process clear, grounded, and human, to help them say yes with both wisdom and joy.

🗝️ Key Reflections

How can I help buyers feel safe, not sold, when it's time to decide?

_____
_____
_____
_____
_____

What visual tools or language could make the offer process less intimidating?

_____
_____
_____
_____
_____

How do I define a "win" for my clients beyond getting the house?

_____
_____
_____
_____
_____

> *You can do anything you set your mind to.*
> ~ Benjamin Franklin

NOTES

DOODLES

CHAPTER 8

OFFER and Negotiation
WIN-WIN Without Overpaying

Once the offer is submitted, **the real art of real estate begins**. Negotiation isn't about out-talking or out-maneuvering anyone. It's about creating understanding, trust, and movement toward a solution that works for everyone.

Buyers often imagine negotiation as a battle; your role is to **reframe it as a bridge**. When you stay calm, factual, and collaborative, you model confidence. And that confidence gives your clients peace. A great agent doesn't push harder; they *listen deeper*.

> *Let us never negotiate out of fear. But let us never fear to negotiate.*
> ~JFK

Your goal is simple: protect your buyer's best interests while keeping communication open, professional, and steady. You're not just writing terms; you're shaping relationships that get deals done.

Reading the Listing Signals and Agent Style

Every listing tells a story, and every agent has a rhythm. The best negotiators read both before they write.

Start with the listing signals:

- **Days on Market**: A quick sale might suggest urgency or competitiveness; a longer one may mean flexibility.
- **Price Changes**: Revisions could reveal motivation levels.
- **Disclosures**: Pay attention to what's shared, and what's not.
- **Showing Instructions**: Tone and detail can reveal how organized or flexible the listing side is.

Then, read the agent. Are they high-energy or reserved? Detailed or brief? Matching their communication style doesn't mean mirroring their personality. It means meeting them where they are. *That balance builds trust fast.*

You and the listing agent ultimately want the same thing; a successful sale and a smooth closing. Approach the conversation as partners in the process, not opponents in negotiation. **When you treat the other side as an ally rather than an adversary, communication flows more easily** and solutions appear faster.

🖋 Writing Clean, Confident Offers

A clean offer doesn't mean stripped of protection. It means complete, clear, and easy to understand. Listing agents love working with professionals who submit well-organized, accurate, and timely offers.

Keep Your Contracts Neat and Intentional

- Fill in every blank and double check all attachments.
- Label documents clearly and in order.
- Avoid vague addenda or handwritten notes that create confusion.
- Confirm the lender's pre-approval letter and funds documentation are attached.

Consider Your Strategy Levers

Escalation Clauses
An escalation clause increases your buyer's offer if another offer comes in higher *(up to a set limit)*. It's a useful tool in competitive markets but should only be used when your buyer is comfortable with the top number and understands the risks. Confidence, not desperation, should drive the strategy.

Seller Credits
This is money the seller agrees to contribute toward the buyer's closing costs, repairs, or to buy down the interest rate. Rather than viewing it as a *"win"* or *"loss,"* position it as a creative way to solve problems or bridge gaps, keeping both sides moving toward a successful closing.

Closing Flexibility: Sometimes timing matters more than price. Offering a flexible closing date, or even a short rent-back period can make your buyer's offer stand out without adding extra cost. Ask the listing agent what timeline works best for the seller and try to align your buyer's needs within that window. A little scheduling grace can go a long way in building goodwill and winning offers.

Contingencies: These are conditions that must be met before a sale can close; protections built into the offer to ensure everything aligns for both buyer and seller. Common examples include financing, appraisal, and inspection contingencies, but in many markets, buyers may also include a home sale contingency, meaning they must sell their current property before purchasing the new one. These clauses are important safeguards, but they can also impact offer strength and timing.

Teach your buyers how each contingency affects negotiation power so you can craft terms that protect their needs while keeping the offer appealing to the seller.

Remind your buyers that the strength of their offer doesn't mean overpaying. It means **presenting an offer so clean, complete, and cooperative that it's easy to accept**.

Helping Buyers Handle the Stress

This phase can stir up nerves, second-guessing, and fear of loss. Calm energy from you will help steady theirs. Encourage *deep breaths, small pauses, and perspective.*

> **"We've done our homework. This offer represents our best, most comfortable position. If it's meant to be, it will be."**

Remind your clients that offers aren't about worthiness. They're about timing, fit, and alignment. When they focus on what they can control *(terms, readiness, and responsiveness)*, the rest feels less overwhelming. **Your empathy is their anchor.**

Counter Strategy & Communication Flow

Negotiations rarely go in a straight line. Counteroffers, addenda, clarifications; it's all part of the process. What keeps it smooth are *connection and rhythm.*

- **Stay Responsive**: Reply quickly to agent calls or texts. Time can kill deals; communication can revive them.
- **Stay Neutral**: Avoid emotional reactions to tone or timing. Keep your language factual, not defensive.
- **Stay Connected**: Update your buyer immediately after every exchange, even if there's no decision yet. *Silence can cause worry; updates build confidence.*

When counters come in, walk your buyers through them visually. Show the differences side-by-side and discuss impact clearly; financially and emotionally. Sometimes the best negotiation move is knowing when to say yes.

Scripts That Strengthen Connection

Bridge-Builder Agent-to-Agent Call Script
Relationships matter and often *make the difference between an accepted offer and a missed opportunity*. It shows respect, professionalism, and collaboration. It humanizes your buyers and sets a positive tone. Open dialogue can build trust, communication, and strengthen your buyer's position before negotiations even begin.

> *"Hi [Agent], I just wanted to connect voice-to-voice. I appreciate how you've presented your listing. It's clear and easy to follow. My buyers love the home and want to make this as smooth as possible for everyone. If there's anything that would strengthen our offer in your seller's eyes, I'm all ears."*

Buyer Expectation Reset Script

> *"Negotiation is about finding alignment. We'll respond thoughtfully and stay true to your comfort zone. My job is to protect your position and your peace of mind."*

Tools That Keep You Grounded

Negotiation Notes Sheet: Track every term discussed, countered, or accepted. Include price, closing date, credits, and contingencies so nothing slips through the cracks. A quick visual reference can save you time.

Counteroffer Playbook: Create a printable guide for your own reference; common counter scenarios, smart phrasing examples, and decision trees for common *"If-Then"* situations. This keeps you poised and professional, even when things get fast and emotional.

🗝️ Key Reflections

How can I create a more collaborative tone in every negotiation?

_____
_____
_____
_____
_____

What communication habit helps me appear calm, even under pressure?

_____
_____
_____
_____
_____

How can I help buyers see negotiation as teamwork, not tension?

_____
_____
_____
_____
_____
_____

NOTES

CHAPTER 9

Under CONTRACT
SYSTEMS That SEAL The DEAL

Once your buyer's offer is accepted, a new kind of work begins... the quiet, behind-the-scenes kind that defines your professionalism. **This is where organization, communication, and calm energy matter most.**

Your buyers have crossed the biggest emotional hurdle; getting the home. But now they're stepping into a phase filled with deadlines, details, and waiting. Every call, email, and update from this point forward can either build or break their confidence. Your role? To be their guide, their translator, and their calm in the storm.

Peace is the product of preparation.

You're no longer chasing the deal. You're shepherding it safely to the finish line.

Let's Sidetrack on a Personal Story

When I first got my license *(waaaaay back in 1999)*, I had never actually purchased a home myself. I was officially trained, licensed, and ready to take on the world as a *bonafide Realtor*. But I had no idea what it truly felt like to buy a home.

Now that I understood the importance of homeownership, I decided it was time to take the plunge and experience it firsthand. I had always loved a*ll things houses*. I'd been tagging along with my mom and aunt to model home tours since I was three. I started drawing floorplans when I was six!

Naturally, the home search part was fun. T*hen came the under contract part*. That's when everything changed.

I was terrified. Every time my lender called asking for another document, I hung up the phone and fell apart, convinced I wasn't going to qualify and would lose the house. It was one of the most nerve-wracking experiences of my life. By the time I made it to closing, *it wasn't joy I felt. It was pure relief*. I was a twitchy, exhausted mess.

But that experience taught the brand-new agent in me something I've never forgotten. *Buying a home can be scary,* even when you know the process. What I needed most was an agent who could calmly guide me through every step without judgment or panic.

That day, I made a commitment that has stayed with me throughout my entire career. No matter what happens, or how the buyer behaves *(or the lender, or the title officer, or the listing agent)*, **I will always be the calm**.

I will *be* the agent that I needed during *my* first deal.

🧭 The Milestone Map

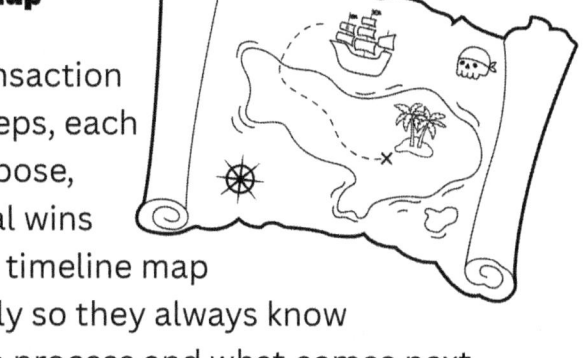

Every successful transaction follows a series of steps, each one with its own purpose, players, and potential wins or pitfalls. Share this timeline map with your buyers early so they always know where they are in the process and what comes next.

- **Earnest Money (EMD)**: Confirm receipt and deposit quickly to lock in buyer commitment. Watch all deadlines to ensure your buyer's earnest money stays safe.

- **Disclosures Review**: Ensure title work and HOA documents *(if applicable)* are reviewed without delay. Encourage thorough reading. Understanding and awareness now prevents conflict later.

- **Inspections**: Schedule promptly; prepare clients for findings and next steps; possible negotiations, price change, repairs addendum, etc.

- **Appraisal**: Coordinate with lender, manage expectations, and stay proactive about timing.

- **Loan Approval**: Maintain communication with the lender to keep documentation on track.

- **Insurance and Home Warranty**: Guide buyers to shop for homeowners' coverage early; delays here can impact closing. Ensure the Home Warranty is ordered.

- **Settlement Statement Review**: Go over the final closing disclosure with your buyers to confirm all expected numbers are accurate before signing. A quick review now prevents the unexpected later.

- **Wire Safety**: Remind buyers to confirm wiring instructions directly with title before transferring any funds.

- **Settlement Day**: Walk your buyers through what to expect at signing. When and where it will take place, how long it is, and what to bring. Encourage them to slow down, ask questions, and celebrate the moment. This is the finish line of their home buying journey.

- **Closing (Funding & Recording)**: Help buyers understand that signing isn't the very end. The transaction officially closes once funds have been transferred and the deed is recorded with the county. Clarifying this timeline keeps expectations realistic and prevents last-minute stress.

- **Keys!** Handing over the keys is more than a formality, it's a milestone of trust and teamwork. Make the moment memorable with heartfelt congratulations, a quick photo, or a small gift that celebrates their new beginning.

Be sure to visualize this path in your **Transaction Timeline** so everyone; you, the listing agent, lender, title officer, and your client, can see progress in real time.

Communication Cadence: Buyer Updates Flow

The under contract period can feel endless for buyers. Prevent anxiety before it starts by setting clear communication guidelines at the beginning:

> *"I'll be checking in every few days with a quick update so you always know what's happening, what's next, and what we might need from you."*

A simple update schedule keeps everyone aligned:

- **Monday**: Touch base with lender and title; verify progress.
- **Tuesday**: Send your "Here's What's Next" message to your buyers.
- **Thursday/Friday**: Follow up on outstanding items or prepare for weekend deadlines.
- **Friday**: Send another message to your buyers.

Your updates can be short; a few bullet points by email or text. The consistency matters most. When clients never need to wonder, trust and calm can continue.

The Problem-Solving Playbook

Even with perfect preparation, surprises can happen. Inspections reveal issues, appraisals come in low, lenders request documentation, or closing dates need adjusting. Your response sets the tone for everything that follows.

Keep your playbook handy:

- **Defects**: Present solutions, not panic. *"We can ask for a repair, request a credit, or take it as-is. Let's review what feels right for you."*

- **Appraisal Gaps**: Show the buyer their options; renegotiate, bridge the gap, or reevaluate price strategy.
- **Lender Requests**: Help buyers stay calm when new paperwork is required. *"This is normal. They're just doublechecking details before final approval."*
- **Timeline Squeezes**: If closing feels tight, communicate early with all parties. A proactive update beats a last-minute inconvenience every time.

Scripts That Build Confidence

Good News Set Up
"We're right on track. This week, your inspection is set for Thursday, and the lender is finalizing the appraisal order. Once that's complete, we'll move into final loan approval. I'll check in again Friday with an update, but text me anytime if you have questions."

Tough-News Framework
Give buyers choices framed around empowerment. *"We have three ways to handle this. Let's pick what keeps you most comfortable."* Start with calm facts: *"The appraisal came in slightly below contract price."* Acknowledge emotion: *"I know that's disappointing. Let's look at what it really means."* Present solutions: *"We can appeal, adjust, or negotiate a credit. I'll walk you through each option."*

Wrap Up

Your value isn't in avoiding problems. It's in leading your buyers through them with poise and solutions. When you show up with your systems ready, your buyers will feel guided and protected.

🗝 Key Reflections

How can I assist my buyers in feeling informed instead of overwhelmed?

_____
_____
_____
_____
_____

Which systems will help me stay ahead of every deadline?

_____
_____
_____
_____
_____

What's one more great way I can bring reassurance and calm into the under contract stage of the process?

_____
_____
_____
_____
_____
_____
_____

NOTES

CHAPTER 10

Closing, MOVE IN & Your Follow-Up CARE Plan

Creating Raving Fans and Long-Tail Referrals

Stay visible, stay valuable, stay genuine.

The deal might be done, but your relationship is just beginning. The closing table isn't the end of the transaction. It's the start of the next chapter for your clients … *and* your business. How you show up in the days, weeks, and months after closing determines whether your buyers *might* remember your name or **rave about you for years to come**.

This final stretch is where gratitude becomes growth. A few thoughtful touches now can lead to lifelong loyalty, repeat business, and a steady flow of referrals. Your goal: to **make every client feel celebrated, cared for, and connected** long after the ink dries.

The Final Walkthrough

The final walkthrough is not just a formality ... it is *reassurance*. It gives buyers confidence that the home is in the same condition they agreed to purchase and that any promised repairs are complete. Keep calm, cheerful, and purposeful.

Script:

> *"This is your chance to make sure everything looks just as you expected; clean, functional, and move-in ready. I'll walk through with you to note anything that still needs attention before closing."*

Remind buyers:

- Confirm utilities are on and functional.
- Test key systems *(HVAC, plumbing, electrical)*.
- Verify repair receipts if applicable.
- Check that agreed-upon inclusions remain *(appliances, fixtures, etc.)*.

Use a **Move-In Checklist** to keep things organized and ensure all items have been checked. End the visit with reassurance:

> *"Everything looks great. Next stop, the closing table!"*

🎁 Closing Day Touches

Closing day is equal parts milestone and memory. You've guided your buyers through every step; now it's time to celebrate their success.

Add personal touches that reflect your care and style:

- **Photo Moment**: Snap a happy *"signing complete"* photo *(with permission)* and offer to text or email it to them.
- **Gift with Meaning**: Choose something thoughtful that connects to their story like a personalized cutting board, local art, a cozy blanket, or a big welcome basket.
- **Welcome Guide**: Provide a booklet of your favorite nearby restaurants, parks, and services.

These little details *create emotional connection.* And this, in turn, *creates loyalty.*

📦 First-Year Follow-Up Care Plan

Your job doesn't end when the moving truck pulls away. The real magic happens in the months that follow. A Care Plan keeps your relationship alive and builds trust that extends well beyond the transaction.

Sample Post-Closing Care:

- **1 Week**: *"How's move-in going?"* text with a friendly check in.
- **30 Days**: Email with *"New Homeowner 101"* tips or maintenance reminders.
- **90 Days**: Quick call to ask how they're settling in.

Seasonal Touchpoints: Send or pop by with a small item of value, like spring maintenance reminders, fall furnace tips, or a *"Happy Holidays"* postcard or small gift.

Housewarming and Community Connectors

You can help your clients feel at home not just in their home, but in their neighborhood.

- **Housewarming Event**: Offer to co-host or drop by with dessert. This is a nice way for your clients to introduce you to their neighbors and brag about what a great job you did.
- **Community Connectors**: Provide your special Vendor list of trusted service pros; painters, landscapers, handymen, cleaners.
- **Neighborhood Groups**: Invite your clients to join local social pages, community events, or homeowner associations.

This goes beyond customer service. It builds community and keeps your name top-of-mind for everyone they meet.

Follow Up Care Calendar

Your **Follow-Up Care Calendar** is your secret to consistency. Plan each touchpoint in advance; cards, texts, pop-bys, gifts, and assign them to specific dates. *Consistency keeps your connection, and your connection creates referrals.*

Your follow-up system is more than a marketing plan. It's an extension of gratitude. Every thoughtful message says, *"I haven't forgotten you."* **And that's what turns happy buyers into lifelong advocates.**

🔑 Key Reflections

How can I make closing day feel more like a celebration than a transaction?

_____
_____
_____
_____
_____

What's one meaningful way I can stay in touch in the first year?

_____
_____
_____
_____
_____

Which tools can help me stay consistent without feeling robotic?

_____
_____
_____
_____
_____
_____

NOTES

CONCLUSION

Buyers for a SEASON
Community for a LIFETIME

Every buyer journey begins with a spark of possibility ... *Is this the home that fits the life we're building now?*

And it ends with a key in hand and a story that's just beginning.

*Clarity → Confidence → Keys.
It's not just a process; it's a promise.*

What happens in between is what defines you as an agent. It's in the systems you create, the calm you bring, and the care you carry through every conversation.

When you **lead with empathy, insight, and structure**, your buyers transform from anxious to assured, from searching to settling, from clients to community. That's the power of your *Client-First System*; it moves them through each stage with confidence.

Your Premium Service Promise

Your buyers may only purchase a home once every few years. But they'll remember for a lifetime how they felt throughout their experience with you. That's why your *Premium Service Promise* is so vital: to be the calm in their chaos, and the advocate who educates them, and the one who keeps their goals at the center of every decision.

This guidebook has given you the systems, scripts, and success resources to serve with excellence. But the heart behind it all is *connection*.

- Be the agent who communicates, comforts, and celebrates.
- Be the agent who follows up when the boxes are unpacked.
- Be the agent who keeps showing up, long after your commission has been paid.

Because that's what turns a transaction into a relationship ... and a client into your champion and raving fan.

The Legacy You're Building

Every time you hand over a set of keys, you're also handing over hope. You've helped someone plant roots, start a new chapter, or build stability for the people they love. That's not a small thing. It's extraordinary.

Your influence doesn't stop at the closing table. It ripples outward... to neighbors, to referrals, to the next family that finds their home because of your care.

When you **lead with integrity, gratitude, and joy**, your name becomes synonymous with trust. And that's how you build a lasting legacy; one home, one client, one heartfelt connection at a time.

Next Steps

Now it's time to personalize what you've learned.

- **Build your Buyer Care Kit**: refine your checklists, update your follow-up calendar, and brand your buyer resources.
- **Revisit your systems**: make sure each step reflects your professionalism and your personality.
- **Show up with heart**: treat every buyer as if they're already part of your community, because soon, they will be.

And when they tell their friends, family, and coworkers about their experience, they won't just say, *"We bought a house."* They'll say, *"We had an incredible agent who made it all feel like magic."*

That's your legacy.
That's your impact.

Buyers for a season ...
Community for a lifetime.

NOTES

MORE MAGIC
Tools to Elevate Your Buyer Experience

These resources are designed to help you put everything from this book into action confidently and easefully. Use them, brand and personalize them, and keep them ready for every buyer you work with.

🤲 BONUS: Scripts for Soothing Buyers

"Calm words create confident clients."

Even the most prepared buyers can hit moments of overwhelm. Financing hiccups, inspection surprises, and appraisal delays can shake even the steadiest nerves. That's when your words matter most.

Here are a few gentle, professional ways to bring your buyers back to center; calm, clear, and ready to move forward.

Why Agency Matters
"My job isn't to sell you a home. It's to protect your interests, your time, and your money. I work for you, not the seller."

Here's How I'll Protect You
"Real estate can move fast, but I make sure you never feel rushed. You'll always understand every document before you sign and every option before you choose."

If Their Offer Isn't Accepted
"I know that's disappointing, especially when you could really see yourself there. But remember, every 'no' brings

us closer to your perfect 'yes.' The right home will meet your needs and <u>feel</u> right. We just haven't met it yet."

When They're Nervous About the Loan Process
"You're not alone. Almost every buyer feels this way at some point. Financing can feel big and unfamiliar. But remember: you have a whole team behind you. I'll stay in touch with your lender and keep you updated every step of the way so you're never left wondering what's next."

When the Inspection Report Looks Frightening
"Inspections are meant to uncover information, not to scare you away. This is just a roadmap of what's real, not a list of deal breakers. Let's take a breath, review the items together, and decide what's worth addressing and what's simply normal homeowner maintenance."

When They're Worried About Appraisal or Value
"The appraisal is just one piece of the puzzle. It's a moment in time, not the whole story. If the number comes in lower than expected, we'll look at all your options calmly and strategically. There's always a path forward, and I'll help you find it."

When the Process Feels Slow
"I completely understand. It can feel like nothing's happening right now. But a lot is going on behind the scenes. This stage takes coordination between lenders, title, and underwriting. I'm keeping an eye on every step, and as soon as there's news, you'll hear it from me first."

When They're Overwhelmed by Paperwork or Deadlines

"There's a lot to sign and track right now, but you don't have to remember it all. I've got you. I'll highlight what's most important and make sure we stay on schedule together. You're doing great."

When It's Almost Closing Day and They're Anxious

"It's completely normal to feel a mix of excitement and nerves right now. You've worked hard for this moment, and everything's coming together beautifully. Let's take it one step at a time. You're almost home."

A Few More Calming Reminders You Can Reuse:

- *"Let's focus on what we can control right now."*
- *"We'll make decisions from understanding, not fear."*
- *"What's meant for you has a way of finding you."*
- *"You're not in this alone. I'm right here."*

 ## BONUS: Working with Buyers Checklist

Set up a checklist for each buyer you work with. This can be online or kept in a folder. Having a checklist will ensure nothing gets missed.

1. Attract & Connect
- ☐ Add new buyer lead to CRM
- ☐ Record lead source *(referral, open house, social, etc.)*
- ☐ Send quick *"thank-you"* or connection text/email
- ☐ Schedule Buyer Consultation
- ☐ Prepare Buyer Packet or digital presentation

2. Buyer Consultation
- ☐ Review agency roles & sign Buyer-Broker Agreement
- ☐ Discuss goals, lifestyle, and timeline
- ☐ Outline process from search to keys
- ☐ Review financial readiness & introduce lender options
- ☐ Provide Buyer Information Binder or digital toolkit

3. Pre-Qualification & Financing
- ☐ Connect buyer with trusted lender
- ☐ Verify pre-approval letter and budget comfort zone
- ☐ Review estimated closing costs & monthly payment
- ☐ Add lender contact to communication loop

4. Search Setup
- ☐ Identify must-haves, nice-to-haves, and deal breakers
- ☐ Create MLS/portal search with customized alerts
- ☐ Educate buyer on market pace and expectations
- ☐ Provide a list of home showing guidelines and etiquette

5. Showings & Feedback
- ☐ Schedule & confirm showing appointments
- ☐ Print or send MLS listings and text list *(with GPS links)*
- ☐ Debrief after each tour (1–10 rating, pros/cons)
- ☐ Track top contenders
- ☐ Send feedback to agents

6. Offer Preparation
- ☐ Review comps & pricing strategy
- ☐ Draft offer with buyer input *(price, terms, timeline)*
- ☐ Review earnest money, contingencies, & deadlines
- ☐ Submit offer and call listing agent

7. Under Contract
- ☐ Track deadlines: EMD, inspection, financing & appraisal, settlement
- ☐ Schedule inspections & negotiate repairs
- ☐ Stay in communication with lender & title
- ☐ Send *"Here's What's Next"* updates to buyer
- ☐ Confirm closing date and walkthrough schedule

8. Closing & Keys
- ☐ Attend walkthrough and verify property condition
- ☐ Confirm utilities transfer & check settlement statement
- ☐ Sign and celebrate at closing!
- ☐ Deliver welcome gift and local guide
- ☐ Post-closing check-in within 1 week

9. Post-Closing Care Plan
- ☐ Enter client into 12-Month Follow-Up Care Calendar
- ☐ Send "Happy Home-iversary" messages annually
- ☐ Provide seasonal homeowner tips & pop-bys
- ☐ Request reviews and referrals naturally
- ☐ Stay in touch as their lifelong real estate resource

BONUS: Homebuyer Information Binder

When you begin working with a new buyer, you will set up an initial consultation meeting to go over what your buyer wants and needs, and what you are going to do for for your buyer as their real estate specialist.

The **Homebuyer Information Binder** is provided to buyers so they can keep track of all homes viewed and all details involved throughout the home search and under contract process.

Include the following sections and forms:

- **Welcome Letter**
- **Homebuyer Questionnaire** – determine the wants and needs of the buyer *(once filled out, this will go to you)*
- **Buyer Wish List** – buyer/s can determine exactly what they desire *(buyer will keep this for reference)*
- **MLS Sheets** – and comparison information for homes viewed
- **Comparable Market Analyses (CMAs)** – done on any homes the buyer might purchase
- **Property Comparison Checklists** – for the buyer to use when viewing homes
- **Under Contract Docs** – copies of purchase contract, addenda, disclosures

Each time you set up appointments for a showing day, encourage your buyers to bring their binder. You will provide current MLS sheets, property comparison forms, and any requested CMAs.

BONUS: Services Guide for Buyers

Create a branded, comprehensive guide for your homebuyers. Use it as part of your initial consultation and leave it with your buyers when they sign with you.

Gather information from your brokerage library or the internet to create pages. This can be an extensive process, so choose pages that matter most to you and begin with them. Then add to your buyer guide as you have time and find more resources.

- **Welcome to Your Home-Buying Experience**
- **Renting Vs. Buying** – Make the Right Choice for You
- **Buying Real Estate** – The Process
- **About Us** – Meet the Team
- **Our Exclusive Buyer Services** – What We Offer
- **Buyer Representation** – Why You Need an Agent
- **The Loan Process** – Application, Steps, What to Do and What Not to Do
- **The Home Search** – How We Do It
- **The Offer** – Understanding the Negotiation Process
- **Under Contract** – What's Happening Now, Behind the Scenes, Next Steps
- **Settlement** – Closing, Funding, Recording, Keys!
- **Time to Move** – Tips to Make Your Move Easier
- **Frequently Asked Questions** – FAQs about Buying a Home
- **Glossary** – Real Estate Terms

📋 Future Homeowner Questionnaire

Create and brand a questionnaire for homebuyers that you can fill out during the initial buyer consultation. Include the following information with checkboxes or space for answers:

- Name
- Address
- City/State/Zip
- Main Phone
- Alt. Phone
- Email Address

- Price range? Payment?
- Qualified by lender?
- Need a lender?
- Monthly payment?
- Need to sell current home?
- Timeline for move in?

- What styles do you prefer:
    - Existing home (age)
    - New build
    - Rambler
    - Two-Story
    - Multi-Level
    - Condo/Townhome

- How many bedrooms?
- How many bathrooms?
- Ensuite?
- Garage size?
- Square footage desired?
- Lot size?
- Outbuildings?

Location
- Location preference?
- Secondary location?
- Important considerations?

Household
- How many in your household?
- How many pets? What kinds?

Lifestyle
- What do you enjoy doing at home?
- What room/s do you spend the most time in?
- Must haves? Would likes? Definite dealbreakers?

BONUS: Moving Made Simple: Agent Edition
Support Your Buyers from Keys to Comfort

Your job doesn't end when the contract closes. It simply shifts. Moving can be one of the most stressful parts of the homebuying journey, but with a few thoughtful systems and gestures, you can help create a seamless and memorable experience.

Before the Move
- ☐ Send a branded *Moving Checklist*.
- ☐ Share your list of trusted service providers *(movers, cleaners, handymen, junk removal)*.
- ☐ Offer a quick call to review utility transfers and *"What to Expect"* for closing week.
- ☐ Provide packing tips and labels for organizing boxes.

During the Move
- ☐ Check in via text: *"How's moving day going? Anything you need?"*
- ☐ Deliver or drop off an essentials basket for moving day, packed with snacks, hydration, paper towels, toilet paper.
- ☐ If possible, stop by the new home briefly to congratulate and welcome them personally.
- ☐ Take photos for client memories and social media.

After the Move
- ☐ Send a note or small gift one week after move in.
- ☐ Schedule your 1-week and 30-day post-close check-ins on your calendar.
- ☐ Share a link to your *Homeowner Resource Guide* or local service directory.
- ☐ Invite clients to join your Community Facebook Group or newsletter.
- ☐ Request a review or testimonial once they're settled and happy.

💕 BONUS: Ideas to Add Extra Heart

- Offer a *"Welcome Home"* pop-by: plant, candle, or fresh-baked treats.
- Host a **Housewarming Giveaway** on social media featuring your clients' story.
- Send a seasonal service reminder (*e.g., "Time to winterize!" or "Spring yard prep"*).
- Add them to your **12-Month Follow-Up Care Calendar** to ensure consistent touchpoints.

BONUS: Calming Practices 🧘
Center Yourself Before You Serve Others

Real estate is emotional. Every transaction carries energy; excitement, fear, uncertainty, hope. As agents, we absorb much of that energy without realizing it. These meditations and mantras are designed to help you reset, re-center, and rise, so you can show up as your calmest, clearest self for every client.

The Grounding Breath (2-Minute Reset)
When to use: Before a client meeting, showing, or difficult call.

1. Sit or stand with both feet on the ground.
2. Inhale deeply through your nose for a count of four.
3. Hold for a count of four, then exhale slowly through your mouth for a count of six.
4. As you breathe, silently repeat: *"I am grounded. I am steady. I am present."*
5. Repeat for one minute or until you feel your shoulders soften and your mind settle.

The Calm Client Meditation *(3-Minute Visualization)*
When to use: Before a showing, consultation, or tense negotiation.

Close your eyes and imagine your client surrounded by warm, golden light. See the light moving between you... a bridge of calm understanding. Visualize the conversation or showing flowing smoothly, with laughter, awareness, and ease.

Repeat silently:

> *"I bring peace into every space I enter."*
> *"My calm creates their calm."*

Open your eyes and smile before walking into the meeting. You've already set the tone.

The Mirror Mantra
When to use: At the start of your workday.

Stand before a mirror, look yourself in the eye, and say aloud:

> *"Today, I lead with love and understanding."*

> *"I am calm, capable, and connected."*

> *"Every client I serve feels safe and supported."*

Repeat these phrases three times. Let it shift your energy before you open your laptop or start your calls.

The Reset Ritual
When to use: After an emotional client interaction or stressful day.

- Step outside or open a window.
- Take one deep breath in for each of the following words:
  "Release... Reset... Restore."
- On your exhale, imagine letting go of any stress that doesn't belong to you.
- *"What's mine will stay. What's not, I release."*

This short ritual clears residual tension and keeps your compassion from becoming depletion.

The Gratitude Close
When to use: At the end of each transaction.

After closing, take one quiet moment before diving into the next deal. Light a candle or simply sit still and say:

"Thank you for this opportunity to serve."
"May this home be filled with love, laughter, and light."
"I release this chapter with gratitude and grace."

Gratitude seals the energy of every deal. It's how we honor the exchange and prepare for what's next.

Add these practices to your daily routine like you do your checklists.

A calm, centered agent creates calm, confident clients.

And that's where the true magic lives.

NOTES

NOTES

NOTES

NOTES

NOTES

NOTES

NOTES

NOTES

ABOUT THE AUTHOR

Donna Wysinger began her real estate career over 25 years ago with a simple curiosity about flipping homes. What started as a personal interest quickly grew into helping friends and family buy and sell properties.

Though she hadn't planned on becoming a full-time Realtor, Donna soon realized that true success would only come by trusting herself and going all in. She immersed herself in the industry, learning every aspect of the business while working alongside top agents and on highly successful teams. Over the years she has worn many hats: listing specialist, buyer guide, transaction coordinator, admin support, new homes specialist, marketing designer and coordinator, new agents trainer, new assistants trainer, and more.

With her strong background in design and marketing, Donna also helped countless agents grow their businesses by creating resources and tools that helped them stand out. Eventually, she partnered with her sister to build a thriving real estate business of her own, using the very systems and strategies she had been developing and teaching. Together, they built not only sales, but lasting relationships within their community.

Today, after more than a quarter century in the industry, Donna has distilled her knowledge and experience into the **Be a Better Agent** community and her series of quick-read guidebooks. Her mission is simple: to help real estate professionals grow with confidence, connection, and ease.

MORE BOOKS in the Mini Mastery Series

If you enjoyed this guide, you'll love all of Donna's handbooks for real estate professionals. Each book is concise, practical, and designed to give you great resources you can use right away. Scan this QR code to explore all of her books on Amazon. *And she's still creating more!*

www.ingramcontent.com/pod-product-compliance
Lightning Source LLC
Chambersburg PA
CBHW071146090426
42736CB00012B/2245